Alive in This World

Other Books by Pamela Haines

Pamela Haines, et al. 2016. *Toward a Right Relationship with Finance: Interest, Debt, Growth and Security.* Caye Caulker, Belize: *Producciones de la Hamaca*

Pamela Haines, 2018. *Money and Soul. London,UK:* John Hunt Publishing.

Pamela Haines, 2021.*That Clear and Certain Sound.* London, UK: John Hunt Publishing.

Alive in This World

Pamela Haines

Producciones de la Hamaca
Caye Caulker, BELIZE

Photo credits
Sycaamore tree: cover, p.1 .... Pamela Haines
Trolley: p. 41 .... Pamela Haines
Strawberries: p. 97 .... Frank Moore
Author: back cover, p. 151........ Drew Martin

Published by *Producciones de la Hamaca*
Caye Caulker, BELIZE
<producciones-hamaca.com>

ISBN: 978-976-8273-26-0 (print edition)
ISBN: 978-976-8273-25-3 (e-book edition)

Producciones de la Hamaca is dedicated to:

—Celebration and documentation of Earth
    and all her inhabitants,
—Restoration and conservation of Earth's
    natural resources,
—Creative expression of the sacredness of
    Earth and Spirit.

Contents

Foreword

Pamela Haines is *alive in this world*, and she is inviting us to join her in discovering miracles everywhere we look.

I have known Pamela Haines for many years, and I have admired her from a middle distance. She has maintained a creative and healing attitude toward the challenges she experiences or sees in the lives of others. When she was rearing her sons, she wrote a column on parenting for the neighborhood newspaper, in which she invited parents to look below the surface and imagine new possibilities. She got to know an African immigrant in her neighborhood, and when that woman returned to Uganda to open a school, Pamela and her husband helped her to fundraise, then went on to visit and build a connection with that community. Her son went to work among street orphans in Nicaragua and there was Pamela inviting her circle to support their soccer games and buy their crafts. Do you find someone to be annoying? Pamela might suggest looking at that person from a different angle.

It seems nothing is too small or too big for her to bring her loving and can-do attitude. Does some problem like macroeconomics seem too big to wrap your brain around? Pamela determined that ordinary folks, not trained in economics, can bring wisdom and understanding and begin to change attitudes and public policy. So she wrote a book about it. Why not? In fact, I think "why not" is often her first response to some seemingly intractable problem.

This book of poetry, *Alive in This World*, gives us a window into the inner processes that inform her rich spirit. Because she is present, open, and observant, beauty presents itself to her. She tells us that she has learned "to look beyond the known, beyond the easy focus point, to train my heart and eye to see the rest" or she observes "and then, one day/my clouded vision clears/I notice what is there," and she finds beauty.

Whether it is trees, or companions on the trolley, or weeds in the community garden, Pamela shows us how to see things as they are. She shows us unexpected beauty, like the trees amid the dull gray office blocks, or the majestic "weed," or the courage, patience, and community on the bus.

She also sees what is awry. "How did beauty/and sunlight/and shade/get privatized?" And, "His pack is like our wealth/worn by good people/who would do no harm/oblivious to how it takes up space/on this earth/swings and hits people/we never see..." And "We all get to choose what we see as weeds."

These poems are filled with seeing and loving and sweating and being blessed at unexpected moments. May you be blessed by accompanying Pamela in her loving observations.

Patricia McBee
May 1, 2021

Preface

I came to poetry through the back door. While I have expressed myself via the written word for as long as I can remember, my preferred form for years was the short essay. This has felt like a supple medium, allowing for the opportunity to mull over a question or an insight without being committed to a larger project. But I remember the time I first had an experience—in our community garden—that just didn't fit the form. It was too striking to go unnoticed, yet when I had finished describing it, I found that I had nothing more to say. It seemed to stand by itself, but as what? Maybe, I thought, this is a poem.

This way of thinking about poetry, as a picture in words, calls to mind the practice of photography. Both require paying close attention, then capturing a moment. As with a photograph, one of the most important decisions about a poem has to do with framing. What am I choosing to include in the picture? What am I leaving out? Yet there are subtleties in photography that are beyond my skill. How do you capture the light in a way that indicates depth? Once you've chosen the center, what can you do to make everything around it point in that direction? How can you make it tell a story? When I wonder why I don't just take a picture and be done with it, I remember that my skill is with words.

Then there's the question of how we choose our own role in the picture we take or the story we tell. I can choose to try to keep myself completely out of the picture so it can stand by itself. Thinking again of photography, and images with my thumbprint in the corner or my own shadow dominating the scene, I know how hard it is to be completely invisible. Alternatively, I can choose to occupy a central spot in the picture, with everything around me becoming increasingly blurry as it fades into the background. This seems hard as well. I am the subject I know the best, but what can I say with confidence that is separate from my surroundings?

Both choices are legitimate of course, but I find myself content as neither an outside observer of life nor its main character. I'm not inclined to linger in an external reality that doesn't include my own experience or an internal reality that doesn't include the larger world in which I'm embedded. It is the interface that captures my attention. On reflection, I find that my poetry is centered in this relationship. How do I make meaning of what I observe? What can I learn from it, about myself, about the world we inhabit together? How does it change me? Beyond relationship, I would hope that my poems provide not only a picture, or a record, or even a story, but a window to the unseen, and to new possibilities.

It's hard to think of a poem that has come to me indoors. The settings have been mostly deeply familiar—the tree-lined streets of my neighborhood of West Philadelphia, the trolleys that take me downtown to work, bits of earth I return to again and again. Most have been composed as I am in motion, working in a garden, walking in the neighborhood, on my way to or from work. Something about being in motion seems to loosen up my brain and allow for new connections.

For me, writing poetry is a gift of pleasure from start to finish. The knowledge that there may be a poem waiting anywhere calls me to pay closer attention to life. When I bring myself fully into a moment that might become a poem, I have the opportunity to be present to all the joy, pain and possibility of that moment. I am opened up. Then I can draw on wells of creativity to craft my words in a way that captures the experience. I can linger with that moment and dig. I can sculpt the experience, cutting away the excess, finding ever-greater clarity of shape and depth of meaning.

When I am composing a poem, I am fully alive. Getting to share my poetry with others is yet another gift.

Pamela Haines
22 February 2021

Acknowledgements

I am ever grateful for the deep and abiding love that my mother, Hazel Haines, had for words, and how she appreciated a good poem. I am nourished by the streak of poetry in my partner, Chuck Esser, that has complimented mine over the years. I am immensely thankful for the encouragement that Judy Lumb, of *Producciones de la Hamaca*, offered when this collection was just a glimmer of an idea, and the care and love that she and Dorothy Beveridge put into every step of midwifing that idea into reality.

As inspiration for this volume, I want to acknowledge my gratitude to all the people of Philadelphia whose lives have crossed mine in ways that gave rise to a poem, especially the transit riders and those whose love for the earth has helped to create and maintain spaces that nourish my soul. Finally, I give thanks for all the trees that I have come to love, both individually and collectively, whose steadfast commitment to life has made so much possible for the rest of us, and for the soil which nourishes us all.

A Home with the Trees

Awe

Sunrise

Pigeon aloft
early light catches her from below,
a flash of golden pink

Sunrise caught in the
tip-top of a sycamore
glowing gold.

Equinox

Winter's end
a tree stands lone and bare
arms outstretched
aglow in slanting sunlight
ready to receive
new life.

Harbinger

A gauzy film of palest hue
lime, pink, mauve
has spread across the grayness of the hills
exquisite harbinger of spring.

Line and space

I've come to love
the strong clean lines of winter
the structure of the trees
revealed against the sky
the interplay of light and dark
of line and space.

The color palette is so spare
it calls the eye
while at the same time resting it—
soft bluish pinkish grays
all etched in black.

Like a fine old movie
in black and white
stripped to its essence
undistracted by the stimulus
that color brings.

I can't begrudge the spring.
Who could?
Yet I will miss these winter skies.

Cathedral

Step out of bright hot sunshine
full of busy sights and sounds
into the cool cathedral hush
of hemlocks leading to the gorge
promise of water in the air
tall ceiling of green filtered light
quiet forest floor.

Autumn gold

The gingko leaves fell today
soft as satin
they cover the sidewalk
line the street
in quiet gold.

Tenderly
gather armfuls
smooth, caressing
fresh and new as fallen snow
to tuck in around
kale and carrots
snug for the winter now
in gently glowing warmth.

Intention

Come

This stretch of road
calls out in many languages:

Be here for the exercise
Smooth roadside surface
flat and humble countryside
of woods and fields
invite a walk.

Be here for the beauty
subtle in its plainness
colors of late autumn now,
soft and sun filled, hard to name.

Today the call is new,
compelling: Come
Be here for community.

Come be with the Pines
whose sharp needles in blunt narrow fans
create an airy solid whole,

Be with the Big-leafed Trees
as their leaves take off into the wind
to meet the earth,

Be with the Birds
a hidden rustle in the brush
till eye picks out the moving brown and white,

Come, bring your species in
your Mammal skin
awareness that is yours alone.
Turn that awareness not away
but toward your place
in this community of life.

Come.

Trees of Winter

I am humbled
by the trees of winter.
I do not know them
yet they are knowable.
In this flat land
each one stands out.
I try to paint them in my mind's eye
as we drive by,
learn them all by heart.

The bold trunks
with zigzagging branches
yielding to bunchy lace,
the slender fingers
that rise and spread out
like a fan,
branches that jut out
horizontal,
those that droop,
some open and reaching,
others smoothly closing
like an egg.

(How do they know
where to reach,
when to stop?)

One could call them all trees and be done—
well maybe in summer
when everything is green.
But now laid bare for all to see
they stand separate, distinct
crying out to be named.

I would know each one.

Choice

Choosing this stop
to get to work
requires a longer walk
but gives a stretch of loveliness—
a park, with grass, trees, flowers, peace.
I soak it in
do not regret the extra block of gray
where office towers soar.

Once past the park my eyes
no longer see.
This block is just
a means unto an end
the price I choose to pay,
invisible.

And then one day
my clouded vision clears.
I notice what is there
and I see—trees.

Slender oak and birch,
ambassadors from living earth
to this alien place,
reach up the narrow canyon
fresh green amidst the gray
unpretentious
brave
resilient
full of grace.

My choice was good—
to take in beauty that I knew was there,
but better still
to look beyond the known
beyond the easy focus point
to train my heart and eye
to see the rest.

Winter beauty

Leaves fallen, flowers gone
time to change my route, perhaps
leave the park to barren winter,
zip to work more speedily.

I look with care amid the grays and browns
find leaves of plants that bloomed
so brightly in the spring
now lovely muted reds and greens, soft golds
Study branches bare against the sky
notice all the seed balls
nature's quiet decoration
Come across a bird
perched atop a tiny tree
singing cheerily.

Next day the muted colors greet my eye again
and tiny balls in towering sycamores
and all the sky
The memory of where that bird sat, how it sang
as clear as day.

These spare lines and quiet colors
call for a sharper eye
alert for smaller, subtler signs.
The need to look more closely
calls out more from me
whets the appetite.
To persevere in face of grey/brown scarcity
makes every find a treasure.
These small beauties fill me up.
The longer route remains my choice
and I am glad.

Relationship

Equality

All trees are the same.
Is this the voice of principle,
or massive inattention?

They are so different.

Some call out their specialness—
the redbud flowers that grow right out of thickest
branch
three kinds of leaves on sassafras, one mitten-shaped
the paper birch, with bark that peels like skin
horse chestnut smooth and round inside that prickly
case.

Others are more quiet but no less knowable
in leaf, bark, color, shape.
Even the sycamores that line the park
are individuals to those who look.

As a whole, trees grow green and tall,
and gift the world with oxygen
but in their parts each is distinct and valuable
as arc we all.

Meeting the Neighbors

We're far from home and much is strange.
Let's meet the neighbors!
(So great to be introduced
by one who knows them all.)

Douglas fir, reaching up and up into the sky
Needles too far to see, but rough bark
and cones with little tongues stand out.
I think I'll recognize Doug fir when next we meet.

Vine maples, slim and sinuous
so different from the maples back at home
a distant family likeness in the leaves.

Hollywood juniper
with that elegant windswept look
that needs no wind--
aptly named, so it would seem.

Limber pine—our host suggests a shake.
I feel the branch's flexibility
will know that hand again.

Alder, tree of the west, you're new to me,
remind me of the beech and birch back home.

Quaking aspen, flat stem on different plane from leaf,
sent quaking at the slightest little breeze
I pick a leaf, examine it
I feel I know you better now, see why you quake.

Cherries abundant, from a large family
meeting you all together
I see the common trait—that simple shiny leaf.
(Your cherries are tart, delicious—many thanks!)

Others to meet, but I am full.
I go about my days in this new place
comforted, more at home.
It's good to know your neighbors.

Oak Tree

This young oak tree bends.
I found it once
near prone across the sidewalk
tire tracks splayed on either side
long gash down its trunk
the victim of a hit and run.

Whose tree?
It wasn't clear.

Neighbors
unknown to each other
pushed it upright
packed the soil
ran ropes to keep it up
clipped the damaged branches
wished it well.

And now years later
it stands sturdily
the long gash visible
but healed
the bend a testimony
to the will to live,
to neighbors' care.

Oak cycle

Through fall
when other leaves turn red and gold
then, knowing that their time is done
gently disengage and float away
oak leaves fade to brown and hold on tight.

Through winter cold when other trees
reveal their splendid bones
in graceful silhouettes against the sky
oaks keep their clumpy ugliness
of rumpled brown.

Even in early spring
when all the world is new
and mists of green are spreading everywhere
those tired old leaves hold tight.

Only when new growth
deep inside the tree
starts to clamor for its turn,
only then do those leaves cede their place
release their hold
and fall.

Branches are bare now
for a short few days
then buds begin to swell
and tiny perfect oak leaf babes
peek out, uncurl,
join the glory of the spring
and start the journey of another year.

Magnolia

The great magnolia down the street
was lured to bloom
by spring-like warmth in February.

Then March brought winter back
with bitter cold that froze the buds
and turned them brown.

And so that great tree stayed
week after week all dead and brown,
till April offered spring again for real.

And now, amidst that somber brown,
new leaves of green are peeping out,
and, high up on one side—a single bloom.

Beech

How could I have lost track of beech?
The beech grove in the woods beyond our house
was sacred play space.
The trees themselves were unremarkable
height medium, leaves ordinary
thin branches that couldn't withstand
our endless will to climb.
It was the space they held that drew us in
a quiet woodsy floor for make believe.

Ranging farther we might find
those magical oak galls (we called them balls)
little hollow spheres of fragile skin,
or tulip poplar seeds that we peeled back and back
until their core—a tiny handled sword—lay bare
in miniature wonder
to bring back to our beech grove play.

Somehow these memories never meshed
with my adult desire to know the trees.
The shape of tulip poplar, tall and straight,
with its round-bottomed pointy-ended leaves
stayed with me. Oak of course.
But as I took in shape and size and leaf,
beech blurred with birch.

I finally had the context and the time
to look with care (and then consult the book).
Beech leaves were larger, shinier, more regular.
The differences were clear. As I look back,
my inattention smacked of disrespect.

And then, by chance, we took a walk in a beech woods
and the memories were stirred
smooth gray bark that drew the eye around,
those thin branches,
and the peace that comes with visiting
a sacred space long lost, now found.

Maple and Oak

Maples take the glory in the fall
with all their brilliant red and gold.
We're glad to give them due.

This year they were outdone.
The great oak round the corner,
usually subdued in plainest brown
broke out in oranges and golds
so deep and rich they caught the sun
like jewels.
(What got into you this year
that made you cut away all modesty
move out in front, take center stage
and shine?)

Next year the maples may assert
their claim to lead again.
I won't complain.
But this year, and in this place,
all the glory goes to that great oak.
I'm glad to honor it,
and witness to the inner fire
that it revealed.

Embodied, at last

These trees evoke my childhood
in songs of vines and fig trees, and the pawpaw patch.
And yet we'd never met.
We had dried figs at Christmas
but my first taste of a fig fresh off the tree
was little short of heaven.
I hadn't known the pawpaw was a fruit
till I scooped my first spoonful from the skin
and marveled at a taste completely new.

Friends, I learned, had both
and I was wild to propagate—
kept twigs of fig in water till they stank with rot
dug pawpaw sprouts that withered to dry sticks.

I persevered. My skill with figs improved
till I had one thriving in a pot in my side yard.
Pawpaws held their secrets tight
then someone else, besotted with this fruit as well,
shared the harvest of her tree
and I got all the seeds, read up,
saved lots in different mixtures in the fridge
planted them all in early spring.

By June I'd given up. Oh well,
failure was my theme here after all. I'd try again.

In mid-July, weeds everywhere, I found some in a pot
went to pull, stepped back, remembered early spring...
the pawpaws had come up!
Who knew it took them months to sprout?
(so little that I know)

They're fledglings now,
songs of vine and fig tree, that old pawpaw patch
now embodied, thriving, in my tiny yard.

Love poem lapse

The trolley is stopped
stuck behind a trash truck, likely—
I don't mind.
I'm gazing out the window
composing a love poem
to the sycamore outside.

I love these great trees that line our streets,
know the texture of their bark
the shape their branches take
just how their fingers meet the sky
the seed balls scattered, nature's quiet jewels,
throughout their crown.

I love these trees in winter, and I
know how they will greet the spring
with tiny folded leaves of April green,
and shade our summer days.

I give myself a mental shake.
This trolley's really stuck—
no one's going anywhere.
I should be working,
making use of this delay.
I pull out the article I need to read,
settle into productivity,
then give myself another shake.

What could be a better use of time
this busy city day
than soaking in the beauty of our world,
noticing my love for that great sycamore
etching it deep into my heart?

On a fruit tree pruning workshop

The melody line dips and soars
through roots, buds, branches
soil, sun, fruit.
The base is a steady
love, love, love.

The buds will lead the way in spring
while the roots are still asleep—
They touch the sun.

Remember the children when you prune—
They need a place to sit
a way to climb.

Feed the trees with a woodsy compost mix—
Think of what they love
and how the fungi nourish them.

I'd cut back on the branches here—
Make it so the sun can find a way
to kiss the fruit.

I would have stayed all day
never mind the standing or the cold
just to hear that song.

I don't remember all the words
I wish I could—
I treasured every one.
But the base stays with me
heartbeat of the universe
love, love, love.

Still Clueless

Pigeons

The pigeons
are pecking at something
under the trees.
What could they be eating
with no bread crumbs
or discarded food in sight?
They seem so happy—
it is a mystery.

I see them again
Happily pecking under the trees.
This puzzle must be solved.
I look more closely,
discover that the trees
have dropped their flowers,
little bunches of nature—
bird food.

Pigeons, it would appear,
have a secret relationship
with trees
that we humans
and our bread crumbs
know nothing about.

Cherries

Fat juicy cherries
on the sidewalk call to me
more wait to fall down.
Did those who planted this tree
know the cherries would be real?

Cherry blossoms

Pink petals fall.
The stuff of poetry:
delicate beauty
soft caress
drifts and clouds
and gentle intimations
of mortality.

But this is not a poem.
It's a squall
a wall of pink
blowing sideways
fierce and full.
Don't be fooled
those flying
blossoms say.
Nature at its heart
is rarely
delicate.

The knock

My eye was caught
by the women's stillness.
Why would she just stand there
in our little city park
in bitter cold
her gaze turned up?

I passed
and then my ear picked up
the hollow knocking
of a woodpecker.

I turned back to join her
looking up
into the tall tall trees.

We never saw that woodpecker
but together
we were witnesses
to life abundant
in a city park.

Trees of Uganda

So many things are new here, and unknown
I watch and listen, try to understand
and then, at times, I'm caught all unawares—

The wind, whose rustle through the leaves
I've always known, feels wrong somehow.
No rustle here: it clatters in the palms.
And tall trees that should be cool and green
unbalance me with flowering flaming red.

It's what I think I know, but don't
that seems most strange.

Dominance

This city park expands
over wide lawns
up through towering trees.
Busy this early morning
with large mammal life
dogs walking, humans running,
it is dominated by the lovely
penetrating call
of one small songbird
in a sycamore.

Loss

Bones of the giants - the woods

There are trees here
not too big, not too small
A woodland of serenity
overlaid with sadness—
everything of majesty is gone.

Only massive old stumps remain
the corpses of our elders
cut down in their prime
their wisdom aborted
now slowly rotting among us
in mute giant reproach.

Nothing to teach us of
how high we can reach
how great we can become.

Bones of the giants - the beach

Torn from the mountain
by raging waters
hurled on the beach
pounded by waves
Great logs and stumps
scoured and smoothed
but undiminished
Bones of the forest
through nature's wrath
now bleached monuments
of the shore.

Woods of Poland

Wildness scares, they say, yet tameness out of place
can send a chill.
This forest, laid out in perfect grid, goes on and on.
How long ago was this land free
to make a forest order of its own?

Fruits

It's easy to love those great trees
of the forest or the park.
but fruit trees call for a different kind of love.
I have a role in their well-being
a stake in their fruit.

Did I plant the right variety
in the right soil, right mix of shade and sun?
And who am I to choose which branch to prune,
        which one to leave?
(It's better when there are two of us.
We step back, envision health, consult on every cut,
remind each other that we do our best.)

And what about disease?
I have no knowledge here, no hidden powers.
Like a mother whose child is sick of unknown cause
I chafe and worry, feel both helpless and responsible.

Perhaps it's not so different with the other trees.
My stake is just so big it's hard to see.
The fruit I need from them is not an apple or a peach
but oxygen, the very stuff of life.

Responsible, but not entirely helpless,
I can gather friends around
envisioning the health of all our trees—
find a place to stand,
a way to act on their behalf and ours.

Inferno

An oasis of serenity no more,
great clouds of swirling dust
roar of machines and men in gas masks
have conjured up a war zone in the park.

The enemy is leaves.
Blowing every blade of grass
blasting under every bush
their goal is total mastery
and barren earth
(which will be covered up next spring
with pricey mulch).

In another universe of possibility
peace and leaf removal coexist:
long-handled rakes and
muscles turned to useful work
bring leaves from grass
to mound around each bush
providing insulation from the winter cold
then breaking down to fertilize the soil.

There's a modest circularity in this
a hopeful sign of things both past and yet to come
acknowledgment that nature and a few strong arms—
no fossil fuels, machines or noise
no pricey mulch—
can do the job with quiet elegance.

Trees in pots

I understand the human logic
of putting trees in pots.
They are easy to contain, to move if necessary.
Their roots don't interfere with things we've built.

But trees weren't meant to stand alone
separated from the earth.
Their roots are meant to mingle—
with roots of other trees and plants
with fungal mycelia, sharing messages and nutrients

Like caged animals
these trees will live, perhaps,
but not with joy.
The cost seems high.
We're all made less.

Private?

Our backyard neighbors
put up a massive wooden fence—
ensuring their privacy
blocking our little bit of sun—
the life of my lettuce and herbs,
flowers and currants
not a concern of theirs.

Our school's neighbors
have cut down the great oak tree
that shaded us all.

I pass the magnolia
two blocks down
a treasure of the neighborhood—
now in full and glorious bloom.
It sits in a private yard—
fills it up. My heart constricts.
What if they no longer chose
to have it there? Cut it down,
as is their right?

As is the right of wall builders
and tree cutters everywhere
on private property.

How did beauty
and sunlight
and shade
get privatized?

Telephone wires

The soaring gingkoes on our street are on the other side.
Trees on our side have to deal with wires.

My heart goes out to all the sycamores
that somehow missed the memo
on the need to keep it short.
They've been chopped and shorn and mutilated
in service to the wires.

The plan to plant with size in mind
has had its flaws as well.
Norway maple's beautifully compact
but its lifespan's short as well.
The ornamental plum is nice,
fall leaves are multicolored, rich as jewels
but it has a tendency to split.
Planted with such hope, they're mostly gone.

Linden was more promising.
Ours was the perfect street tree
great for climbing and for shade
till, heedless of the memo, it grew into the wires.
The first time it was cut back, it survived.
The second time, years later, was just too much to bear.
All those brutal cuts, made in the name of mastery,
cost our lovely linden first its beauty, then its life.

I'm thankful for the gingkoes
free from the tyranny of wires.
There's nothing in the linden's place for now.
We've talked of peach or cherry, but I may go with sun
to bless the little nursery in our side yard.

Nicaraguan shade

The pain of poverty shows in this hot land
in butchered trees, chopped to armless trunks,
new growth cut off before its time.
They're cutting down their shade to cook their beans.

Gifts

Celebrating Easter during a pandemic

The sunrise service that I love,
in a meadow by the riverside,
putting our gathered attention
to the end of night
and the coming of a new day,
was not to be.

Instead, I climbed to our roof—
moon to the west, over the great church dome
sunrise to the east, through the skyline—
and settled in to witness
the coming of the light.
And it came.

Back down, my early morning walk
led me round the park
and to the city garden that we share.

Under the peach tree
that I planted years ago
and has yielded so abundantly
I found a tiny seedling poking up—a peach!

As I looked, I kept on finding more—
life in abundance,
unexpected and unearned
ready to grow, to nourish and delight—
an Easter gift to warm the heart.

Gingko Trio

1. Imprint

Early morning
picking my way through ice, snow and mud
to a long-delayed mammogram
spurred by a friend's discovery of cancer
eyes to the ground.

Suddenly—
an abundance of
delicate fossil imprints of gingko leaves
pressed in the cement,

Conjuring an image
of sidewalk repair men
lovingly pressing leaves
into the fresh new surface.

Smiling, looking back
to see the bare tree
with its unmistakable silhouette,
imagining the scenario
unfolding without human intervention.

Which gives more pleasure?
It is a mystery
a gift.

2. Catching the light

Out at sunrise and
the topmost branches of the gingkoes
are aflame with light.

At the corner, looking west
all the treetops are aglow.
Turning south
where buildings block the sun
the trees are bare and plain.

When I arrive back home
the gingkoes are just trees again.
their halo now a memory.

By some amazing chance
I'd caught the light.

3. Leaf play

I eye the gingko leaves
fallen all at once in mid-November rain.
Raking them up, so warm and rich
tucking them in among the plants,
has been a sacred task.
When will I have the time?

Later, coming home, I hear a squeal of joy.
School girls on their lunch hour break
have made a pile of leaves
gathered armloads
flung them in the air.
That joyous laughter lifts my heart
and I don't rush right in
to rake the leaves away.

Next day there is more:
A group of boys and girls have made a game
of throwing leaves.
When have I ever seen them mix
in outdoor play before?

With leaves and laughter in the air
my heart is filled
and I will wait to use my rake.

Tough nut

This nut protects itself.
An outer rough green skin, when penetrated
dyes the fingers brown
(try to explain that stain on fingertips
and under nails at work).

The hard nut underneath
calls for hammer (car tires in a pinch).
Finally the meats
picked patiently from tiny rooms inside—
the taste—there's nothing like it in this world
(with so much work involved
these nuts can only trade in love).

How do the squirrels get in
(hammers we don't know of in their mouths)?
They leave the nut shells, hard and round
with holes and furrows conjuring
a little creature face.

One day we find those shells,
look up to that great tree,
then take the time to study saplings
sprouting up nearby—black walnuts all.

Some nuts had kept away from those sharp teeth
found strong connection to the earth,
an inner life force pushing through the shell
to root and grow—
the knowledge of a towering tree
complete somehow in that hard nut.

Maples

This post and beam construction was a joy—
my sister and our teenage sons
together, sawing, chiseling
seeing this small building take its shape—
a sugar house.

Late winter and I make the trip again
up north and through the mountains,
then the final hill, the crest
and there the valley opens up below,
in beauty any time of year,
now blanketed in snow.

Six great maples line the road
beside the house,
a few more in the woods nearby—
provide all that we need.

Sap drips into buckets, buckets fill.
We haul them to the sugar house,
fill the wide flat pan above the fire,
add more wood.

But our main job is to wait
outdoors in winter, warmed by fire
taking in the glory of the day,
be present to the gift of maples
as their sap transforms
to nectar of the gods.

Bones of the giants - the forest

The roots of tall trees form an arch
high enough to walk through
marking the height where tiny seedlings
once took root on some great fallen log,
taking in its richness, growing up
reaching roots around and down
until they reached the earth.

Smaller trees and mosses
grew around the log as well,
thriving on its nourishment
in rich community.

That great log has gone back to the earth,
this verdant tunnel left to mark its place.

Sycamore

The sycamore is bathed in sunlight
stone church behind in deepest shadow—
Light on dark.

Then a line
where the branches reach out
past the church to open sky—
Dark on light.

The tree is whole, unchanged
The background that we choose
makes all the difference.

Bathing in wood air

We all know that a walk in the woods refreshes—
great trees, bird calls and breezes
pungent scents of earth and pine.

Yet our senses fail to name the greater forces
here at work.

Mushroom threads—mycelia—
weave a network underground
sharing nutrients at the root
helping those great trees to thrive.

And all those trees give out
not just the oxygen
that we forget to thank them for
but other subtle essences
(named now by scientists, thus real)
that nourish us.

We are bathing in wood air
as they say in Japanese
deep in the molecular life of the trees
breathing in the benefits of
living in an interspecies web.

Hemlocks

I love these hemlocks
gracing pond and woods and gorge
round a cabin far from home.

They live in mortal danger now.
A bug, so small it needs a microscope,
can suck the life from those great trees
(I watched the gypsy moths eat up the maples
so I know).

It has no native predators
but they can be brought in and bred.
We found someone who does it,
made a date, carved out the hours,
went hurtling through the night
to meet him in the woods.

(His cousin runs the show.
He'd started with her in his teens.
Now saving hemlocks is his life.)

We walked the land.
He spoke of seeing miles of forest
devastated, dead and gray.
"Your trees are healthy still,"
he said. "You're not too late."

We made the plan, then turned around
and traveled all those hours back to home
and ordinary lives. All seemed unchanged,
but we could breathe more deeply now,
a jewel of good news in our hearts:
Maybe we can do this thing
and save the hemlock trees.

Park in August

Early morning at the park
in the cool before the blazing heat
joggers
dog walkers of all sizes and shapes
homeless men waking up
stretching
all mostly alone
under the great canopy
of sycamores and cicada song.

Evening at the park
as the day cools
A row of chess players
connected and intent
couples on picnic blankets
two older people
doing their tai-chi routine
a drumming group--
all drawn together
under the great canopy
of sycamores and cicada song.

Commuter Encounters

Prologue

Trolley love

I have to say I love the trolleys
Humming quietly along our streets.

Buses roared in one summer
as track was repaired farther west—
Bigger, noisier, smellier
uglier and more crowded
all at once.
Transferring to the trolley
at the portal to the tunnel downtown
was like stepping into spacious peace.

These trolleys are sleek and new...
Well, let's say
I remember the old ones.

I saw a movie once
where trolleys lent historic color
to evoke a time long gone.
They were just like those
I used to ride to work each day—
I felt proud, obscurely gratified.

They do break down sometimes
get stuck behind stalled cars
fill to overflowing with commuters
and noisy school children,
can be just a means of
getting from here to there.

A bike might be the smartest way
to travel those miles
for some people, some times.
But after that, for my money,
it's the trolley.

Witness

Roots

Standing in the trolley
looking down
at tops of heads
and hairdos,
I see to the roots.

Passion, shared

A thin old man waits at our stop
his clothes defying current style
an instrument across his back—
perhaps a violin.

The trolley comes
we bunch up at the front
no space to move on back.
My mind is who-knows where
when words begin to pierce my consciousness.
He's talking music with the man behind the wheel
camouflaged till now by uniform,
invisible to me.

Yet they can see.
Race and role irrelevant
they're passionate, intense, informed
delighted in this circumstance
that throws them in each other's path
for this sweet interval.

Hands

All I can see
is brown hands
and a catalog

Brown hands turning pages
full of lovely dresses
on lovely white models.

The hands
don't seem angry—

Perhaps
that's the part
I can't see.

Bracelet

No seats on the subway
Looking down
I see the heavy steel bracelet
on a young man's ankle.

I'm shocked and shamed
like seeing a brand on the forehead
or scars of a whip.

I'm sure there are some who'd say
that it's benevolent
far better than a prison cell.
I'm sure they'd say the same
about the brand
or the whip.

Quartet

Four old ladies two by two
four different hats
(sensible on this brisk October morning)
four bags on laps
hands folded on top
four stories to tell.

Their faces are attentive, kind—
lively talk and laughter
flow between the pairs.

They have troubles
I'm sure—and flaws
and yet, and yet
this sturdy foursome
shouts out
(in their old sensible way)
all that is right
on this October morning.

Curves

As he leans on the pole
his whole body curves.

Straighten up!
Try a little!
Have some pride!

He moves to get off.
The curves remain

and the voice in my head
looks for a place
to hide.

Carrying the load

This family has a tale to tell.
There's something not quite right about the boy.
He's not all there.
The mother tends him tirelessly
her patience like an ancient rock
worn smooth by time.

An older son sits quietly with yet another boy.
A glance, a word shows just how much
she counts on him.
How heavy is his load
how gladly shouldered?

As their stop comes, a comment shows
the third son too is slow.
It seems too much to bear.
They don't complain.

And what are we to do
but open up our hearts,
carry our load lightly and give thanks
for all that's whole?

Layers

Neon laces
wide striped knee highs
paint-stained tights
two petticoats, short skirt—
vision in black and white
crafted carefully
from studded toes to studded upper lip
calculated to offend
the prim.

From a handbag
screaming out defiance,
she pulls a mirror
studies, then applies
a tasteful shade
of color to her lips.

The urge to defy
covering or covered by
the ancient training to attract,
and underneath the paint
the black and white,
a human being
not yet visible.

Pink Shoes

Swirly hot pink plastic shoes
Orange baseball cap
with sparkly golden spider webs
A snazzy dresser for sure
this large middle-aged woman—
and a bright place to rest my eyes
on the trolley going home.

Sunday morning
swirly hot pink plastic shoes
catch my eye.
This time the hat is fuller
brown with golden pattern.
She is reading her Bible—
not just a colorful distraction
but a neighbor.

Cheekbone

I can't see beyond her cheekbone
or hear his words
yet there is warmth in her face.
She is full of open
receptive attention.
He talks and talks
to that steady attention.
He is a lucky man, I think.

Then there is a change.
What did he say?
Her face closes.
His tone cajoles, jokes
She is not won over.
He explains, dismisses.
That look of warm regard is gone,
replaced by wariness and hurt.

And I, who have seen no mouth or eye,
heard no word,
know nothing
but the changing slant
of a stranger's face,
feel an aching loss.

Alone at dawn

Before dawn
the streets near empty
I wait for the trolley.

Alone in this still world
I cling to the schedule's promise,
need it to come.

I imagine the trolley empty
but for a few hardy
pre-dawn travelers,
and I wait

Till it appears over the rise
like a ghost in the night.
The built-up tension of the wait
dissolves.
I will make my train.

Gratefully I step up
to great quiet
as I expected—
but the trolley is full.

It is full
of resignation, patience,
endurance, sleep
as its inhabitants
make their daily way
to the early shift
and I go on my adventure.

Fragments

His costume:
suit, black shoes, computer
knit hat topped with pompom—
youthful exuberance
poking through pin-stripes.

Fine slender fingers
T-shirt cut to show the shoulder
Hair short, topped by a bright red mop
Tasteful tattoo at nape of neck, new beard.

Two slim hands hold tightly to one pole
bright pink of sweater peeking from each sleeve
two different shades of skin
two separate girls.

Using the window for a mirror
she applies lipstick with care.
Looks forward, turns again
and adds a little more.
The goal—a perfect face.

A thin young man in army surplus stands
balancing a big china bowl of cereal
eating methodically
through jerks and stops.

She takes the steps
two at a time in office pumps,
not in a hurry—just full
of the stretchy energy of life.

This couple's talk is easy, intimate
she tall and blond, he compact and black.
I would know more and listen shamelessly—
they're speaking French.

Each a fragment of great poetry
I'll never know.

Connections

Blessings

My day goes better
when I call to mind
this chance to offer a brief prayer
Bless and keep
Bless and keep
for each one
getting on
or off
the trolley.

Missing

Hurry down the block
miss the trolley
head on, then stop
remembering
trot back home
retrieve the missing wallet
miss the trolley yet again
catch the third one
come across
a long lost friend—
no longer missing.

Wild man

The free seat
is across from a wild man
Bushy hair and beard
layers and safety pins
a certain unfocused look
Someone to avoid
whether from pity
or from fear.

Yet I know him
His brother knew my husband
years ago.
He is brilliant
knows more about world
politics than most
would be homeless
I'm sure
without his brother's help.

I greet him
and we chat
Mostly I listen
He goes on about Korea
US nuclear policy
carries stacks of dog-eared papers
eager to inform
hoping
(in vain I am afraid)
to make a difference.

I'm self-conscious
as we talk
torn between embarrassment and pride
at claiming a relationship with one
who has slipped so far from normalcy,
who looks so wild.

Trouble

A man named Travis has troubled my soul.
Thin as a rail
gap-toothed
eager to please
he rings our bell
looking for work
or a token at the end of the day
to get back to the shelter.

I have more than I need
but hold my giving plans dear.
They have not included
his presence on our doorstep
time and again.

I feel coerced
ill-used
ungenerous
His need is greater than anything I can give
Why has he chosen
our step
as his refuge?

When he tells of plans
to move far away
I am glad.
I can hope his life will be better
knowing mine will ease.

Months later
on the trolley
I look up and see Travis.
In this sea of strangers
we are like old friends.
He has much to tell
of travel
his mother's death
troubles he's seen.
I am glad to be there
provide a container
for his story.

No matter
that he breaks my peace
he is someone
I have come to know.

Trolley Talk

It started with my lunch bag
and, perhaps, a smile.
How did I know that store—and how did he?
Then on to other things.
He teaches high school
is feeling tired
If only they could start the day with prayer
they could focus
be less out of control
It may not be enough these days
We used to value family
And the culture is so hard on them—
there's so much greed.

Ahead of us more talk
had taken root
between seat and aisle.
The man was joking
looking for a wife.
Said he worked hard every day
would love some good home cooking.
The woman said you need a maid.
To find her man
she'd rather look in church.
This one wouldn't be there
He worshipped chicken
Deep dish macaroni.

This easy banter
Flowed back to reach our quiet earnestness
And we all smiled.

Trophy

We met on the trolley.
I was so proud
to strike up a conversation with
this young man from Iraq.
It was a triumph
a stand against caution
and all that separates.

We stay in touch
attend an event on Palestine.
He teaches at a local college
has a toehold here.
Later we chance across each other
on the street
exchange a warm hello.

Months later
his name pops up in my mailbox
suggesting tea.
His time is very open…

We meet, talk politics
I ask about his life.
He's lost his job
alone in this country
scared and vulnerable
reaching out
to those he might call friends
including me.

A sobering reminder that
connection on the trolley
may not be an end in itself
but only a beginning.

For what we get

I've had no use for picky eaters
who ask for help on the street
and should be thankful
for what they get.

And then I got to know one—
always there between the trolley stop and work.
I liked his cheerful greeting,
moved cautiously from eye contact and smile
to the occasional dollar,
from introductions to chat.
(He learned my birthday,
sang out on the street,
and made my day.)

I learned his bagel of choice.
It is a small thing to buy
the ones he prefers
and make a sandwich
as I make my lunch.

Cinnamon raisin?
he asks hopefully
With cream cheese?
Of course, I say.
At least he gets his way
in one small thing.

Roller-coaster

As I prepare my lunch
I make an extra sandwich
feel connected, and well used.

Leaving the trolley I feel for it.
I've left it home—
stupidity!

Scanning the street
I see no sign of him
in his accustomed spot.
What a relief
that I won't have to disappoint.
But then
he calls to me
from the next block
and now I must apologize
for my mistake.

But we have time to talk.
He's worried about his health.
is all alone and craves
a friendly, listening ear.
and so I listen, care, and feel
connected and well-used.

Rain choice

Out from work
and into steady rain.
I'll reach the trolley quickest turning right
yet there's a sandwich
lying heavy in my bag.
I missed my homeless friend
on the way in,
won't find him if I take the shorter route,
may not find him anyhow.

I hover as the rain pours down
and then turn left
at rest in that good choice.

And then I find him,
give the sandwich
chat beneath an overhang—
a spot of brightness
in the midst of all that rain.

Bus and train interlude

The #42, Part 1

The trolley tunnel is closed.
A rumor flies—
someone was on the tracks—
but no one knows.
We're sent off to take the bus
disgruntled and late.

I never ride this bus.
It loops around
so inefficiently.

This time I have no choice.
I too must loop
and meaning grows before my eyes—
in hospitals.

First in the loop, the VA
then Children's, HUP.
At each stop old men
workers, family groups
crowd off and on
before we head decisively
downtown.

We need our loops.
Straight lines, it seems,
lack something in
community.

The #64 Bus - To be at home

I huddle in cold rain
waiting for the bus that does not come.
At first I was sustained by novelty,
consciousness of doing right,
joining with the ones who have no choice.

The rosy glow of virtue
has worn off. I miss my car.

The trolley ride to work is not the same,
so quick and easy.
No one of sound mind
would take a car downtown—
no place for virtue in that choice.

The bus arrives, moves on, fills up—
an old man, wheelchair bound,
old ladies struggling with grocery carts,
canes, packages, small children, crates of food.
These folks are tired and poor.
I feel cocooned in privilege.
I'm not the one who needs a car.

A mixed lot on the trolley,
we are bound in common cause—
all are off to school or work, or coming home.
Here I have no sense of commonality.
I cannot grasp the shape of people's lives,
am not at home.

Stepping out of this strange world
I find the rain has eased.
The bus moves on.
The ground is solid underneath my feet,
the streets familiar, houses known.

How can we have such intertwining worlds,
so close and yet so separate?
I think I need to ride more often on this bus
not for virtue (though it is the better choice)
but to find our common shape—
to be at home.

Round Trip on a Spring Sunday

It can be done without a car
long walk up 47th
starting with
a feast of April beauty.

Grace to grit
pocket park
bright plastic gym set
in a trash-strewn lot
a few cheap chairs.

The el with its view
of close-up decay
vista of flat rooftops
housing for the workers
factories long gone.

City's edge
trolley through inner suburbs
yards full of life
a girl on her way to the mall.

Stop in the woods
walk through farther suburbs
polished lawns, to the goal
a quiet retreat.

Then back.
Two moms with strollers
bevy of little girls
exciting game of station master
at the trolley stop
(they don't get on).

Old woman with grocery bags
getting off midway
stops to adjust her purse and load
as she heads home.

Police at the el
sight of a creche
on a porch roof
passionate talk
in heavy accent
embarrassed children.

Crowd at the pocket park
menacing somehow.

Down 46th
Picket-fenced vacant lots
Vietnamese cookout
spilling into the street
as evening falls.

A car would have slipped
swift and sanitized
through April beauty
saved time
missed the world.

The 64 Bus, Blessing net

I climb aboard the 64
could continue with my book
decide instead to pay attention,
offering a prayer of "bless and keep"
for everybody on the bus.

The woman in the wheel chair
taking up four seats,
The teens in their school uniforms,
The young mothers with small children,
(ethnicity changing with the neighborhoods,
Black, Spanish, Southeast Asian)
The old Chinese man who struggles with each step
The white man with a caved in face,
as if he'd received a bone-crushing punch,
The older woman who is late to work,
worrying that another wheel chair
will be maneuvered into the bus
slowing her down still more,
The young woman on the phone beside me
pregnant, supporting a man who doesn't do his share
wondering what comes next.

On the way home,
old men with bags,
young women with scarves,
the crossing guard
with his bike on the front,
but mostly the small boy slumped in the seat
across from me
unhappy, maybe tired or sick,
with a father who watches but does not touch.

They are there with me
I welcome them, hold them
then look around and they are gone.
The net of blessing on a bus
is full of holes.
Nothing can be known for sure
about what good it does
except that I am better off for holding it.

Conductors on the R5

I thought conductors
took tickets, called stops, opened doors
got paid, went home
But these guys claim the train
as sacred trust.

A woman on the platform is slow
disoriented, perhaps
not sure where to go.
The conductor is patient, kind
stays till another woman,
her gestures confident, comes
and he is free to go.

Another time
he stands at the station
waiting, holding the train
his hands wondering.
Who does he expect?
She arrives breathless
he relaxes, and we move on.

Later, the old woman
of an elderly pair
talks and talks.
He inclines toward her
listens patiently.
She stays behind
as the old man climbs on.
Is the conductor to watch out for him?
I'm sure he will.

Though I need nothing this time
am not a regular
I feel tenderly held
infinitely cared for
in hands I can trust.

After taking tickets, calling stops
opening doors and tending their flock,
do they go home proud?

Reverse Commute on the R5

The city's underbelly lies exposed.
No tidy lawns or fine facades
but the ugliest of raw backyards
junked cars in narrow lots
derelict buildings
rusted industrial
detritus.

My light skin stands out
on this morning train ride
from the city.

Then the shabby inner ring—
old suburbs, industries
some sites spruced up, recycled
others less accommodating
hulking witness to a time gone by.

A lone woman gets off
and hurries down the street.
Does she clean?
Are her employer's hours
as unyielding as the train's?
Do they match?

Then new homes
industrial parks
gleaming prosperity.

Riders empty out,
a bus fills up
headed for a corporate park—
convenient, I suppose
for those who have no choice.

A field once graced with cows
now sprouts mansionettes,
the land transformed—
what once produced
now houses wealth.

These mansions do not warm our hearts
there is no rush of gladness
to be nearing home—
just a day of work
and then another long commute.

Train choice

Hoping for a quiet ride
my heart drops
when the man behind me
starts to talk.

The business call is boring.
I can block it out enough to work.
His next call is different—
a lover, it seems,
and all is not well—
harder to blur into background noise.

The road to anger beckons.
He has, after all,
invaded my space
cut up my peace.
But where would it end
and what would I gain?

I choose the other path,
work to the accompaniment of
a sad man's story
take it in, hold it
and silently wish him well.

Misinformation

The automated voice on the el
is seriously off track.
As we travel east
below the city center
stopping at 15th, 11th, 8th
she announces neighborhood stations
heading west:
Huntingdon, Dauphin, Berks, Girard.

We have to shut that voice out
focus on what we see and what we know
trust ourselves to find our way.

It's disorienting to exist
within a narrative so false
spoken with such authority.
At least here, on the subway
we're a savvy bunch.
We don't get fooled.

The #64 Bus, Unexpected gladness

I fret about the snow
the icy streets as yet unplowed
the on-street parking trauma—
it's no day to take a car.

Then I remember—
there is a bus.

I walk four easy blocks
where I am picked up
chauffeured
delivered worry-free.
I step out
light and unencumbered
a block from where I do my group.

But there is more.
Off the very same bus
steps the janitor
(he'd gotten on not far from home—
I'd never known).
We chat about the bus
our common neighborhood.
For months I'd looked for ways to get to know
this man.

After my group, he jokes
talks me out of a donut
says I'll miss my bus—
the bus we share.

I do.
Sitting on a wall in bright sunshine
I write Valentine notes
waiting
in unexpected gladness.

The #42, Patient courage

The trip across town on the bus
is slow and clogged with need.
One wheelchair takes the place
of all the front seats on the right.
A few blocks farther on, another woman
in another wheelchair waits.
Four old people in the front stand up
without complaint and shuffle back
negotiate walkers, ease into new seats,
willingly made free for them.

We go past the hospitals
crawl in all the traffic they pull in.
Lose one wheelchair
at the Children's Hospital
(does she have a loved one there?)
the second at the VA.

A new crowd gets on—
weathered lives,
oxygen tank in a shopping cart.
Young mother and child
are leaven to all this age.

An old woman with a cast
that has blocked the aisle through all of this
eases slowly, painfully to her feet
settles in a seat freed up
by the departing chair.
Blocks later she gets up again
and slowly, slowly
works her way to the door.
A man (her son, perhaps) is waiting
there for her.

There's courage on this bus,
patience, and community.

Dilemmas

Back of the Trolley

Moving back
I slide through the bulge in the middle
to the space in the rear
where young men lounge,
spreading out limbs and packs
over empty seats
daring anyone to sit.

I understand the impulse
for those who have been oppressed
to defy the powers that be—
to take up space.

Should I
show my solidarity
and stand?

Or would that silent, distancing respect
be seen as fear,
give angry isolation
victory?

Is it better (braver)
to call on their humanity,
expect common courtesy
and
politely
claim a seat?

Neither way can make right
what is so wrong.
Yet I would choose
the back of the trolley
where I can sit (sometimes)
be human
and not forget.

Standing

I am content
to stand
polishing a line of yesterday's poem
about those
who lounge in defiance
taking up space
in the back
(there are no empty seats today).

The young man
sitting below
could be such a lounger
is dressed for the part.

But I don't attend
My mind is elsewhere.

His question
catches me by surprise:
Would I like his seat?

Hair

From my seat
I see heads and hair
have leisure to examine

Afros, corn-rows, twists
wigs, hair pieces, extensions
hair that's permed, straightened, dyed—
a dizzying array.

My questions have no end—
What shapes the choice?
What is the process?
How was it done?
Which parts are real?
Can you sleep on it?
How long did it take?
How long will it last?
(How much did it cost?)

How do you ask questions
when not knowing
brands you so indelibly
as one outside the fold?

I watch a man's fingers
loosen cornrows
with the patience of generations.
I see hundreds of braids
coming undone.
I am a pro at braids
itch to get my fingers in,
restore order.

My contacts with African hair
I realize up till now
have been brief and
fraught with feeling.

A black friend
in my white suburban school
rushing to catch the bus
her hair undone—
I braid for her
in wordless urgency
knowing without being told
the vulnerability
of that untamed bush.

An Ethiopian lover
the thick spring of his hair
part of the strange magic
of a time
steeped in impermanence.

I seize on conversations at work
hair stories
Learn enough
to ask a little more—
chances to move beyond
scared child
fragile lover
trolley voyeur.

Relationships grow.
The time comes when I get the chance
(no artist yet)
to work my own fingers
through this rich black medium.

Taking up Space

I find the last empty seat
watch idly as a young man
moves back
finds someone he knows
turns to chat.

His backpack turns with him
barely misses
the head of an old man
seated below—
I squirm.

The talk is lively
My eyes are glued to the pack.
It moves
brushes the man's hat
He hunches forward
too old and tired to protest?
It swings back
bumps lightly
a dance too painful to endure.

I call out to the young man
invite him to notice
He moves immediately
offers an apology
clearly
he had no idea.

The apology
of such a nice young man
should help
But I am galled
by that black hole
of unawareness.

His pack is like our wealth
worn by good people
who would do no harm
oblivious to how it takes up space
on this earth
swings and hits people
we never see, leaving them
to hunch and duck
if they are tired
or generous beyond measure—
to rage
if they are not.

Quiet Torture on the #34

He sits in the aisle
fiercely guarding the empty window seat
just because he can.
As the neighborhoods change
the trolley fills.
A young white woman
works her way to the back
asks for the seat.
In the ungracious shuffle of moving aside
the straps of her backpack
brush his face.
His muttered *What the fuck!*
vibrate with passion
at the world's injustice.
Her angry, ill-used, *Well I'm sorry!*
offers no relief.

(Even if the ripples of slavery
had been foremost in her mind
and her heart full of love,
could any apology
by a stranger
on the trolley
in the early 21st century
suffice?)

Side by side they sit
in silent indignation
and blame.

Then it gets worse.

A friend of the woman's
greets her from the aisle
across the head of this angry young man.
They chat pleasantly
about work, home life
ordinary things that just require

a bit of education, money
order, security, direction
nothing much
if you have the means.

As this easy conversation
rich with privilege
fills his space,
he reaches in his pocket
pulls out a lighter
flicks it on
then adjusts it
so the flame rises higher.
Sends that flame rising
over and over again
till he gets up to leave.
and each is freed
from the torture
of the other.

A search for bad guys would yield nothing.
Claiming an empty seat
silent angry endurance
chatting across a stranger
do not suffice.

Yet the evil of inequality and separation
filled the back of the trolley that morning,
foretold danger
called out for the courage
to lance festering wounds
deal in awareness and rage
throw our hearts over the chasm--

Perhaps not right there on the #34
but not far away.

The Seat

I am tired
and grateful for a seat.
Then a young woman
with a baby strapped in front
finds a place to stand by me
and breaks my peace.
I'm not so young and my feet hurt.
I hope in vain that someone else
will make the move
or she'll get off.
I try to calculate
who feels more tired.

Finally I give it up
and offer her my place.
She sinks down without a word
strokes her baby, gentle and intense.
Will there be no smile, no word?
Will we stay separate,
locked privately in our two worlds?

Yet in that movement something shifts.
The old man squashed beside us is not shy.
He says how beautiful the baby is.
Another, just a girl, has to agree.
Once started they chat easily
breaking down the walls.
We all now sing the beauty of the child.
The mother's face, so closed, begins to open
spreading a circle of warmth around that seat
including us all.

Buddies

I may have to leave this seat.
There's much I can tolerate on the trolley
but an assault from right behind—
loud hyper-confident male arguments
second guessing pro coaches and athletes—
seems more than I can bear.

It's awkward.
As I consider my options
the conversation shifts.

Do you have a date for the weekend?
A softness moves in.
intimate and vulnerable
Then classes, homework
teacher strategies.
These are school boys
helping each other make it through.

As they pass my seat to leave
I see the first one
fair and open faced
then the second
dark and more restrained.
Their friendship is worth cherishing.

Affinity

Pants
with a knife edge crease
Blazer
Browns and blues
all speak of casual good taste
(African hair)
University perhaps.

Another—
Long overcoat
Graying hair
Voice with just a hint
of Europe
Colleagues, I would guess,
easy with each other.

Then,
standing to get off,
Youth
Low-slung baggy pants
Crotch at the knees
Layered t-shirts.

We could clump
those knife edge creases
with the baggy pants
together
on the basis of
the wearers' skin,
their hair—
But would they be at ease?

And if the baggy pants were on a
White
Child of the streets
would that Europe-inflected overcoat
choose them
or those more familiar
Browns and blues?

Stand?

I'm offered a seat more often
on the trolley these days

I could take offense
refuse to be consigned to elderhood
stand up for my ability to stand.
This defiance
this refusal to be labeled
as unable
resonates.

Yet who am I to stand stiff-necked
against the kindness of strangers,
assert my lone fortitude
against community?

(In truth I would be glad to have a seat.)
I am disarmed.
I sit
and am glad.

Moral workout

Window seat
last place to sit on the trolley
guarded fiercely by a woman of color on the aisle,
no eye contact as I approach
no movement, no offer.

Having me stand
gives her a point,
helps even the score
in a game that was stacked against her long ago.
We're both in the game
I never chose this hand of cards
wish I could lay it down, start fresh.

There's that ugly history
the cards we can't lay down
the challenge to concede a point
by standing.

But if a million older women on a million crowded buses
stood when seats were free
would justice roll?
Would this young woman hold her head up high?
I see no winning in this game,
no good move to make.

I call instead on common courtesy
excuse myself, squeeze past her thick reluctance
say thank you and sit down.

I like to get off early,
a longer walk but quieter, and through the park.
She sits immovable, perhaps asleep.
Will I squeeze past her once again
or wait, forego my walk
and get off at the transit hub?

This seems an easier choice—
throw away my high card
of the choice to take a nicer walk
so she can rest.

Next stop, I gather bag and gloves
get ready to excuse myself again
She wakes and asks me where we are
and leaves, amazingly not mad.
I follow her, a little limp but not regretful
for this moral workout
on the morning trolley.

Blessings

Going Home

I stand at the front
of the trolley
looking back.
Two by two
they sit
patiently waiting for home.

So many faces
serene, tired, still
a few in lovely talk
each with a story
I don't know—
a random slice
of the human race.

I see patience here
and kindness
Could we live together?
Would I find
a friend?

This fleeting congregation
touches my heart
and I step down to the street
refreshed.

In crowd

A long stretch of
wet sidewalk cement
had proven irresistible.

Now when I walk
to the trolley I pass
first Nick
then Bob
and then a chicken (boldly drawn)
with the Cleveland Cool Kids
closely on its heels.

My step lightens (every time)
I have to smile.
I'm part of the crowd
they've invited me in—
Nick
Bob
that perky chicken
and all the cool kids
from Cleveland.

Bubbles

A child is blowing bubbles
from the back of the trolley.
Tiny, they float and drift.
People turn, smile.
"I thought it was snowing" says one
and laughter ripples
through the car.
Singlehandedly
a small child
has lifted our spirits.

Cold and kindness

Slip out from under covers
leave that cozy nest
for broken-furnace winter.

Outside is colder, with a biting wind.
Pass up the car's warm ease for trolley
choosing for equity and the earth.

Walk then wait. Our numbers grow
in turned up collars, quiet deepening chill
broken by a new arrival
middle aged and black
shabby, rounded, warm with laughter
greeting a white man
crisp in uniform, measured and erect.
My mind puts them in roles,
opposing sides, and yet
they chat with ease and mutual respect.
The white man says he still can't go to malls
the black man has no job, needs trauma help
they must be vets
the bond of war too great to break
on class or race or other circumstance.
A place inside me loosens in their warmth.

The trolley comes.
A couple shuffle in and take their seats
one carrying his oxygen,
their bickering cannot obscure
how they rely on one other or their care.

Late for Sunday service but already filled
with kindness in the midst of winter cold.
Home, to find the furnace man has come,
and we have heat.

Giving

A scruffy young white man
calls for attention on the subway
asks for help.
I'm not inclined to give.
I can't help but wonder if he chose this fate
if begging has become his work.
I avoid eye contact,
not happy with the situation or myself.

A small hand reaches out
a quarter is exchanged
I turn to look.
A black boy, maybe ten
a little down and out himself
or so it seems
has found it in his heart
to be more generous.

The man, a blur, moves on
The small brown hand
is etched behind my lids.

Baby power

End of the working day
headed home in the growing dark
to disappointment and struggle.

A bright-eyed baby on the trolley
catches my eye
and hold me in his clear-eyed gaze.

As we look into each other's eyes
slowly, slowly, I can feel corners of my mouth
being drawn up—I have no choice
and we smile.

Good Air

A woman with a damaged mind
sits in the front seat of the 34
silent for the most part when alone
loud, insistent, inappropriate one-on-one.
Regulars, for the most part
know to steer clear
giving up the chance to sit
for peace of mind.

An unwitting traveler at times
is lured to sit and trapped,
a victim to her storm
of loud demands.

But there are times of unexpected grace
when someone takes that seat
and knowing or unknowing what's in wait
is kind.
The flood of words, slurred and hard to understand
meets patient warm respect.
Demands are courteously turned aside.

The world shifts
as a sweet fresh breeze
wafts from that troubled seat
tensions ease all round
and everyone drinks deep
of that good air.

Red light

Hurry past the food truck
toward the trolley
rich aroma wafting.
miss the light
am drawn back
to that tantalizing smell,
Inhale its goodness
savor every big deep breath
of ethnic fast food,
meditate
on what costs money and
what satisfies.

The vendor wonders what I want
I have to say I've taken it—
without pay.

Then hear my name
a long-time neighbor
known since he was small
now moved away
buying from the truck.
asks how I am
sends regards to the block.
We smile, remember
all those years.

The light has changed.
I cross through biting wind
savor all the life lived well
in that brief red.

February thaw

Coming home
the commuters look different.
They have sprouted with flowers
balloons
bright packages—

Edges soften
hearts peek out
love that must be
there every day
made visible.

And I
hardened foe of consumerism
am touched
this Valentines Eve.

Humanity

Early evening
and the trolley is crowded.

A mother and little girl
given a seat
A very tall man in the back
head almost touching the roof
holding a small baby
relaxed, content
The arm of a man around a woman
the woman's around a baby
in close circles of caring

Love is present in this house.
Peace prevails.

A Home with the Earth

Prologue

Finding earth

This city house is spacious on the inside
shade in back, concrete in front.
Where to get my bit of earth?
Break the concrete
haul my mother's compost pile—
create a patch of brightness
but so small.

Over the years I come to see
the neighborhood has more—
community garden, rich with possibilities
neglected public flower beds nearby
all crying out for care.
Others around me share this love
for soil and growing things
in jewels of projects
some still waiting to be found.

I wanted earth. I find I have enough.

Cultivating

Private property

Wisteria, fragrant and lovely
won't grow in my garden. I discover
that a neighbor has succeeded.
I stop, rest my eyes, lift the cluster
of purple blooms and breathe them in.
In that moment the wisteria's beauty
and fragrance are all mine.

Farther on I see pansies
by the cemetery gate. They are new
their bright cheerfulness
an unexpected gift, now mine.

Just beyond is a bit of earth
backing the trolley tunnel
planted with hope, now overgrown.
I stop with trowel and trash bag
glad to give back a bit of beauty.
This land owned by the city
is now mine.

What is this business
about private property?

Volunteers

I love the sunflowers, urban volunteers
year after year dropping their seeds
so a new generation can delight all who pass
with their bold beauty.
No flower we've planted here compares.

I love my tiny plot
with its thin pointy strawberries
that melt in your mouth
rhubarb overflowing
turnips we eat from tangy leaf tips
to fat lavender root when they are new
carrots, lettuce and kale.
I have raised them like children
they have done well and I am proud.

But oh the sunflowers!
Profligate in their generosity
they are beholden to no one,
abundant volunteers.

Margins

I like to weed from the edges
claiming everything they enclose.

Most of the show is at the center
rich and beautiful, calling for attention.
But if you tolerate weeds at the margin
they grow in.

Starting at the margin
is a decision
to have everything.

Color

What gift to give an aging mother, living far away?
The pleasure of a crossword puzzle shared
tasty meals assembled from not much
sparkling surfaces,
But when I leave, what will last?

Arthritis in her back makes it hard to bend.
Her rock garden has suffered from neglect
edges blurred by grass and weed, all overgrown
a few brave pansies struggling on.

The soil is rocky, hard to dig
and yet it's small, so progress shows.
As lines grow sharp and spaces open up
the barren earth calls out to be filled in.

We venture out with color on our minds
come back with pink petunia,
blue lobelia, pansies in all shades
paint in the spaces.
Take the quiet background colors
that were at home among the rocks
tuck their babies into cracks,
create a vibrant picture—
the first thing that she sees
each time she opens up the door.

Cultivating confidence

At a public flower bed nearby
a nasty weed has taken hold.

I pull out plants
whose roots spread out and sent up shoots.
I know there will be more,
come back to get the ones I missed
and come again.

This is a strong resourceful foe
and yet I rest in confidence
that I will win,
not the first time or the tenth—
this weed's tenacity
and hold on life call for respect—
but if I do it long enough
the flowers will prevail.

(Though other weeds
will come of course—
the larger work is never done.)

I like this stand.
Can I transplant it—
lend this steady confidence
to other parts of life
where weeds are choking
things I love?
Learn to not succeed
the first ten times
and still go back?

Some things are worth the effort
no matter what the odds,
and with a win in sight
it's not so hard to find the time.

To see that distant win
requires the confidence
that I know best
when gardening.

Lenten rose

The hellebore, or Lenten rose
is new to me—
deep mauve and ivory
in bloom before the daffodils,
now planted in one corner
of our park.

A bitter winter hid the ground for weeks
park lovers picked their icy way
or stayed at home.
But now the corner with the hellebores
has been revealed—
awash in trash.
I pass it twice, in pain.
The third time, in the rain
I find a plastic bag
and pick it clean.
The corner now is theirs alone.
The hellebores can shine
in all their quiet loveliness.
My eye can rest
and I go home
more hopeful, and refreshed.

To feed the people

The crew comes at seven.
Already hens are chattering contentedly
with each new egg.

(As a guest of this farm family
I can choose my hours
don't have to come at all
but they are short staffed today
and I am drawn like a magnet
to this work.)

I start in the lettuce
each head a work of art
to be placed reverently
in the box.

Then washing by the barn
joining the crew in cleaning salad mix
leaf by leaf by leaf
saving rejects for the chickens.

(Now I know the work behind those bags
we pick up in the grocery store.
Who gives thanks
as they pour that bounty out?)

Four pounds of basil.
My host buries her head
in the bag and breathes it in.
How did God come up with that one?
she asks.

A farm worker from years past
comes with her child to shop.
Together we cut parsley, make bouquets.
The little girl holds the rubber bands
and helps to count.

Sugar pod peas. I'm on my own now.
Three hundred feet of bending.
I try sitting, kneeling—
bending, unfortunately, is best.
But peas fill the bucket, more than enough
and just a taste of farm labor.

After lunch I help the woman shop—
Regular peas (snap open the shell
roll your finger down to loosen the row
and taste a fresh gift from heaven)
Broccoli, a great bouquet of Swiss chard
red, green, yellow, white.

We need ten pounds more of chard.
(I'm tired, on vacation, would quit
if I weren't so clearly needed.)
I pick, wash, weigh, have only eight
trudge back for more.

The salad mix order is short
more to cut, more to wash
leaf by leaf (a soft rain starts)
then load the truck, all tired to the bone
and send it off to stores and restaurants
to feed the people.

The reason for all this love
all this work.

Efficiency

Part of me
(the old part)
is sharp with impatience.
I could do this transaction
in a quarter of the time
a tenth.
There's work to be done
I haven't got all day.

The other (newer) part
would extend this moment
buying dry-root strawberries
(five kinds)
from the young man
at our new neighborhood nursery.

We chat.
He gardens across the river
volunteers at the same
urban farm I love
with the same black farmer.

I have visions of
young black men
from all across the city
finding this farmer
soaking up the lore
of earth and growing things,
reclaiming roots.

We knit a connection
while he sorts and packages
these roots for me.
Why would I ever
want this time to end?

Discerning

Decisions

What to pull out in this trolley portal bed?
My childhood training says poke is a weed,
its berries are poison, dig it up.

I dig out the big one that droops
and mars the front of the bed.
The one on the side is newer, graceful
Foot on the shovel, I pause.

The berries hang, hard green and menacing
and yet I know them well. When they are ripe
they make lovely purple dye and ink—
remembered treasure for a child. I let it be.

Milkweed is a weed
tall, flat and coarse. Dig it up.
But I have eaten milkweed blossoms
in dusky pink bunches when they are new.
The curvy gray pods open to reveal
a magical nest of soft silk
and seeds that blow free, light as down.
Those ugly leaves provide the food
for monarch butterflies
(would there be monarchs here?
we would be so honored).
I let the milkweed be.

Portal

Walking home I pass the trolleys
full of commuters bound for work.

Covered in dirt, shovel in hand
I am of a different breed.

Yet I too ride the trolley in a skirt
hair up, to a job downtown.

There at the portal I could be either.
Can anybody see that I am both?

Naming

Not clearly a weed, I watched it grow.
then finally bloom
in pinks and purples,
a lovely plant.

We'll leave the larkspur
said a fellow gardener.
Larkspur. Now I knew its name.

Showing the wildflowers
she'd grown from seed
a friend asked if I knew
that tall plant. Larkspur, I said.

Larkspur. She considered.
I don't know if I'll keep it or not.

We all get to choose
what we see as weeds.
I like it when they have a name.

Bedtime

*The workshop will be on
putting your garden to bed for winter—
all gardeners are encouraged to attend.*

But wait!
My garden isn't ready to go to bed.

Carrots, kale and swiss chard
are still going strong.
New lettuce has come in thick.
Turnips just keep getting fatter.

They are awake, alert, full of life.
Why can't they stay up a little longer?
(And why do other gardens
need such an early bedtime?)

Whose job?

My goal is a refreshing early morning walk.
The park is quiet, cool and lovely
till I reach the corner where path meets street.
A new planting that I'd noticed earlier
has now been overgrown with weeds
marred by neglect (neglect by whom?)
Someone should be taking better care.
Who might that someone be?

Do I love the park?
Do I know what should be pulled?
Do I have a little time—right now?
I stoop and start to weed.

Weeds of my childhood

We pulled pigweed from the garden
when I was small.
You had to get that long red root,
which we would polish sometimes till it shone
imagining the pigs.
Neighbors in the plot that's next to mine,
from Africa, now grow it as a crop.
They prize the greens.

One day, long ago, before I knew
as we prepared the garden to be judged,
their plot all overgrown,
my son and I pulled those red roots.
It makes me hot with shame.
To me it was a weed.

When I was little, purslane was a weed.
We pulled it out, incurious
about those tiny pear-shaped leaves
those fat round stems just tinged with red.
And then, the shock of finding
purslane seed for sale.
Purslane as a chosen crop!
Tasty, they said, and good for you.

Never had it crossed my lips in all those years,
but they were right. Now when I find purslane
coming up I welcome it
knowing I will have a valued salad green
when lettuce wilts from heat.

When I was little, plantain was a weed.
It marred the lawn
with big round leaves and seedy stalks.
Its one redeeming feature was the stem:
scored with thumbnail,
gently pulled apart it would reveal
four strings of a guitar, a childhood magic trick.
But in the lawn we pulled it out,
no place for magic there.

But now I've learned the magic is no trick.
Just pick a leaf, the native people say,
chew to make a poultice, get a balm
for many ills that plague the skin.
They treat plantain with reverence.
Can I do otherwise?

But what of all the truths
I learned when I was small
of what is good and what is bad,
where virtue lay in pulling out
all but the crops we chose,
in our straight rows
and our neat lawn?
It was so simple then.
How do I weed my garden now?

Dandelions

At my house
dandelions were not allowed.
You could find
mold in the fridge
dustballs in the corners
stacks on the surfaces
But dandelions were dug out
every year, one by one.
A lawn, after all,
is no place for a weed.

(We picked them in meadows
slit and curled the long stems
braided flower crowns
blew on those irresistible
fragile spheres
but that was different.)

And so I dug them steadily
from yard and garden
habits strong
virtue and vigilance combined.

One Easter we are gifted
with a salad of first greens.
Weeding his garden, a relative
had found too many dandelions to resist.
It was a labor of love, he said
all that washing.

As I savor the sharp taste
I feel a dissonance with my past
and give thanks for this love of a weed.

Ranking

It rained last night.
The curly kale, bejeweled in early morning sun
lets loose its raindrops
at the slightest touch,
all a miracle, as I work
to find and kill the beetles
in their bold and striking color
that can ravish such a row as this.

Then morning glories
majestic in deep purple blue,
heart stopping loveliness,
climbing with abandon on the berries—
pull them off, discard in heaps
a loveliness that threatens
fruit we hold more dear.

We have our reasons for these choices
yet I wonder, who are we
to rank the miracles of life?

Learning

Revelation

April
I don't know the flowers in this community garden
but I'm on a crusade to eradicate a weed.
It sends out runners that love to intertwine
among the roots of other plants.
I dig them out of something that is probably a flower
then they come back, and I dig again.

May
This plant spreads too—I'm pretty sure it's not a weed.
Week after week I tease the bindweed from its roots
sometimes dig a whole plant up to get it free
then plop it back in the earth and hope for rain
(there's been lots of rain this spring—it rains again).

June
I'm tired of these plants that still harbor my foe
but I am determined to beat this weed.
The plants are bigger, getting ready to bud.
The bindweed that remains (less now)
hides in the foliage, coils up a stem.
I uncoil tendrils patiently.

July
Returning from a week away, I am confounded.
Those plain little plants that I fought with,
got mad at, was tired of
but never gave up on (barely)
are now adorned with stunning bursts of
black-eyes Susans
one of my all-time favorites.

Possession

In the common front garden
I grew used to finding that noxious weed
maintaining a serenity, a clearness of purpose
the bindweed is here and I can dig it out.

I left my own little vegetable plot
tucked away in the back
to manage on its own.
Seeds had been planted
just needed to grow.

Then one day in my tiny bed
amid fragile little carrot greens
and new lettuce
I found a hearty bindweed plant
bursting with life and energy
ready able and eager, it seemed,
to take over everything.

No serenity here.
I felt personally attacked
assaulted, violated.
Partly it was because they were
so new, so vulnerable
But mostly it was because
this was mine…

Stung

Bees in the echinacea blossoms
what a thrill!
I'm sure they were there last year
but I never noticed.
Spending hours in the front garden this spring
I have gotten to know the bees.

I feel a kinship. We both love the garden
my labor helps them eat, their labor
gives my work more meaning.

So I was not prepared the other day
amid the jungle of enormous sunflowers
to be stung. As I yelled and jumped back
I saw a half a dozen buzzing angrily around
an unseen nest.

It hurt, but even more, I felt unseen myself.
Didn't they know I was their friend?
How could they be so indiscriminate
so without thanks?

My upset couldn't last.
After all I knew that these were wasps
no relation to the honey bees
in the echinacea flowers of the front
(what human arrogance to see them all as one!).

But more, this was no place for gratitude.
I was doing work I had chosen.
We were all living our lives
as best we knew how.

There is no one to blame, nothing to change
(though I will take more care in the future
among the sunflowers).

Greens

Africans in the garden plot that's next to mine
are picking greens.
The leaves remind me of the vines that
now are running riot in my sweet potato plot.

I ask. They are indeed the same.
You eat them? I'm incredulous.
We cook them up with onions
for our stews, they say.
Sweet potatoes can be bought
for cheap in any store.
A bunch of these will cost five dollars though,
shipped in from miles away.
We grow them for the leaves.

I have to say, I'm growing mine
for all that rich and orange meat
still hidden underground,
but let me try those leaves—
so dark they must be full of iron and vitamins.

Sauteed with leeks and chives
parsley, celery, all homegrown,
stewed with fresh tomatoes
they make a tasty sauce.
Who knew?

I want to tell the world—eat sweet potato leaves!
That's why we all need Africans
to garden with.

Facing fear

On a country walk in the fall
my eye is caught by scarlet and gold
low along the roadside.
I know this beauty. Poison ivy.

Weeding this spring before the leaves were out
I was caught by it unawares
and ended up with a full body case
of itching torture.

I would flee, have always fled before
but this was our garden, my work.
Gathering up resolve
(and gloves and plastic bag)
I pulled (so carefully) found more
fought fear and great discouragement
pulled again—and was unscathed.

Hatred, dread and a one-point plan
to keep my distance from this menace
were transforming to relationship.
I found I breathed more freely.

Poison ivy still is not my friend
but on a crisp October day
its brilliant reds enrich my life.

Altar call

Each time I pass this little altar
to Breonna Taylor I am moved.

The flowers, bought with love
arranged for beauty
all the candles lit with care
the fierce determination
that this woman will be loved
and not forgotten
Each time I pass I take it in
and yet still feel apart

Till I recall that I have flowers too.
I pick some from our common beds
find a jar and water
place my little offering with reverence
in this place of public grief
and feel more whole.

Eats

The harlequin beetles and I compete
over who will eat
my precious crop of kale.
I am bigger and stronger
can crush them with a pinch—
when I am there.
They are more numerous,
and they never stop.
This morning, a battle raged:
beetles devouring kale,
me crushing them by the dozen,
as a swarm of mosquitoes
undaunted by my size
or drawn to it, perhaps,
sucked on my blood.

Wood chips

This little pile of wood chips caught my eye
six weeks ago between the sidewalk and the street.
Were they trash or treasure of this house?
I eyed the pile, could make good use of it.

But when neglect had shown that it was trash
the days had grown so hot that moving it
would be a sweltering task.
Other outdoor needs called urgently
for those cool early morning hours,
and so the little pile remained
and life went on.

A big rain finally came and broke the heat
It brought another change as well:
mushrooms sprouting from the wood chip pile!
Life had, indeed, been going on.
Fungal threads—mycelia—had taken hold
somewhere within the pile, and spread and spread
till finally, dense enough, they pushed the
   mushrooms out.

Without a doubt this pile is treasure now.
It's come alive, is on its way to join the soil
that, with the water and the sun,
sustains us all.

I may dig into this pile or I may not.
Already it has nourished me
with its reminder of abundant life.

Sharing

Neighbors

We'd met before.
He was sleeping behind the flower bed
at the trolley portal when I came to work.

I felt awkward, intrusive, but not afraid
so I dug while he slept.
When he woke, stretched, rolled up his things
I wished him a good morning as neighbors do.

The next time he was leaving as I arrived.
We exchanged a nod and a smile.

This morning I am not prepared to find him
sleeping so close, hardly concealed by a bush.
Will we always share this space?
I worked here long before he settled in,
have thought of it as mine.

I tiptoe around, digging quietly
my back to him when I get close,
trying to respect his fragile bedroom wall.
Then sounds of rustling, the smell of a cigarette
his start of a new day, shared.

Garden help

I met her at a green skills workshop in the dead of winter
she had garden dreams for the children, but no space.
I made some introductions,
got her number, said I'd love to help…

A young woman friend of my son's
lives in a blighted part of town
doing what she can to make a garden grow.
With dreams of bringing life into a barren place
I said I'd love to help…

I found a morning, and her blighted neighborhood
and lot—and deep rich soil.
No need for compost here, or elbow grease
Someone else had done the heavy work.
I helped her weed.

A friend came by. She's making gardens, raising food
in neighbors' yards—they get a share, she sells the rest.
I took her card, and said I'd love to help…

I call the green skills woman—learn she has her lot!
She's also learned from master gardeners
found a funder for her dream, greenhouse and all.
She's done the work. All I can give is pleasure at her news.
We say we'll stay in touch.

I learn the backyard farmer wants perennials—
flowers to go with food.
I have plants to share, write a note,
wonder if I'll hear from her.
The days go by. I dig and weed and plant familiar ground
long past the days of rubble and abandonment.

She writes back, thanks me for my warmth
says they'd love my extra plants!
I gather pots and compost, dig out black-eyed Susans
that have multiplied so happily and overrun their space.

And that is all: those black-eyed Susan plants
a little weeding in good soil
some warm words and encouragement—
a paltry set of offerings
compared to my great dreams
of helping nurture life in barren ground.

I could despair, am tempted to, and yet
there's goodness all around
and seeds of help are mysteries.
I cannot know how long they take to sprout
how much they spread, what kind of fruit they bear.
It's mine to cultivate the longer view,
to sow and water, and to wait
trusting good seeds in good soil to grow.

Old friends

She showed me her garden, ruefully.
A grand plan of past years
had succumbed to back pain
and discouragement.
Maybe she could get my help
with just one thing?

A big poke weed, fat and sassy
offered insult, a slap in the face
every time she looked out back.
Digging it out was easy, and
one thing led to another.

She pruned, I pulled, we talked
and a garden she hadn't seen for years
grew before her eyes.
Her pleasure grew before mine.

Encounters

The woman hailed me from the sidewalk
Was the president of the garden around?
They had spoken about a vegetable plot.
She was from Africa, brightly clothed
I was covered in dirt.
She wrote her number on a bit of paper
I took a corner, hands encrusted
shoved it in my pocket, called the president that night.
Later the woman saw me, thanked me for my help.
She now had her piece of earth.

A young woman asked, *Will you be here for a while?*
If a taxi comes for my mother and me
could you say we'll be right there?
A taxi from a garden seemed an oddity
but I watched and hailed him when he came
then went to look for them amidst the plots
hurrying as the meter ticked. Her mother was old.
They thanked me. I was thankful for their ride.

A man called from a roofing truck across the street.
Was it for me? Did he need help?
I put my shovel down and went to ask.
No, he said. *I would never have whistled that way for you.*
But he knew me, had seen me working there before.
It was a neighborly exchange.

A woman with three children stopped to look.
Together we admired the bees
busy in the echinacea blooms.
I wondered, were these honey bees their first?

The mailman stopped to chat.
We need this kind of beauty
in the neighborhood, he said.

Dreams and stones

Sunday morning trolley diversion
I change my route and
take the longer walk to catch the el
see one train go by, know there's time
to detour to the vacant lot nearby—
a garden dream of local youth.

Their dream called out to me
I'd come one day to help them work.
The lot was stony, bare, unpromising
We scraped away and rock piles grew.
Two young men sweated at my side
pulled out iron rod, concrete, more rock.
Could this poor place yield anything
but stony pain? My heart went out to them.

Three weeks have passed. What will I find?
Long rows of rock line narrow beds
where good soil has been added.
Thin onions plant, fat cabbages
peek through a covering of hay
perky and content.

Dreams and sweat have made their mark
in this bare place.
Glad for my choice of route
I climb the steps to catch the el.

City harvest

Graterford Prison
heart of urban despair
old greenhouse brought back to life
Large hands
unused perhaps to nurturing
put seeds in tiny pots
tend sprouts and fresh new growth.

Then say goodbye to healthy seedlings
with regret, perhaps
and send them out into the world
where neighbors work in city garden plots
to plant them in good earth
weed, water, watch them grow.

Our garden is among the hosts.
The man who works our City Harvest plot
is finding unexpected joy
in growing food to give away
(I tend the flowerbed in front).

Early on a Saturday
I find him there at work
hoping for an extra hand
and gladly drop my private task
to help in harvesting
kale, collards, broccoli.

They've grown so big and beautiful
and when I put them in the tub
and gently push the great leaves down
until the water covers them
they shimmer with silver lights
in beauty that astonishes.
It is a mystery, a sacramental task.

I add a batch of flowers for the alter
and off they go to the little storefront church
where good food will be greeted with delight
and given out to those in need.

A sacrament, in truth, at every step
from their first start as seeds
in gentle hands at Graterford.

Soil

This vacant lot is vast, a gap where two great houses
used to stand, now hemmed in by poverty.
A lovely family tends it for the children in their care
and the neighbors who need beauty and good food.

Our garden's flowers have spread and spread.
These new friends are precious and I long to share.
One great carload and a morning's work together
fill the few raised beds, the soil hauled in
from far away by this good man,
each hard-earned shovelful a kiss, a promise
of more nourishment to come.

I would fill this lot with flowers, growing so abundantly
born to multiply. Yet in this packed debris
a shovel cannot penetrate. What's needed first is soil.
My little compost pile, even if I gave it all away
would be a speck in this vast lot—and I have need of it.

My easy generosity has foundered
on the hard slow work of building up the soil.

Heat wave

Saturday morning
in the garden
at the crack of dawn—
finesse the heat wave
(watch the sunrise).

Others come
to water, weed and harvest
sweat
all sturdy urban gardeners
who know
you can't avoid the weather
if you want the food
but you can be smart
about when you're out.

We chat
just neighbors
tied close this morning
by the choices we have made
about the weather
and the earth.

New life among the daisies

The heat wave has broken
the morning is blessedly cool.
I've chosen to deadhead the daisies
down at the trolley portal—
a lovely show in weeks gone by
now they look unkempt and full of death.

As I snip, I learn how low to cut
so barren stems don't poke up high
but not below where new buds still might come.

I get a cheerful greeting
from an old man walking by
and am reminded of the vet last year who said
he'd learned a whole new love for flowers
walking by these beds each week
from the trolley to the VA hospital.

Starting the last bed, working from within
I face the sidewalk
notice all the people in their v-necked uniforms
who minister to veterans
but may have troubles of their own.

Perhaps these beds can be of some small use
to strengthen fragile hope in need of evidence
that life is good and can be beautiful,
to play a role in nourishing a loving heart,
assaulted on so many fronts in these hard times.

I leave the daisies looking perky, full of life.
The plants can concentrate on flowering now
and there'll be beauty for another week or two
for those who take this early walk to the VA.

Turnip greens

The turnip seeds are old
I plant them all—and all of them come up.
I thin and eat them once, then twice
but turnip greens are not my favorite.
Third thinning, and the pile is high.
These eager seedlings are good food.
Can compost be their highest good?

A friend counts on my tomato plants each year
growing them for the children in her care.
I bring her tomatoes, mention all the turnip greens.
Give them to me, she says. *I'll be glad to cook them up.*

Early next morning I wash that great pile of greens
bag them up, bike in the beauty and the cool
and give them to my friend.
Through love of growing things, friends, southern
    cooking—
life has found a way, and all is well.

Gifts

In our big shared garden
digging baby black-eyed Susan plants
to give away
a Mexican neighbor offers me cilantro
and I go home with four sweet plants
to tuck in with my herbs.

Then, carting pots of flowers
that have spread out of their beds
to share with neighbors hungry for color
in the barren apartment beds
that line the street,
I greet a gardener
who turns out to have
sunflowers to spare,
and digs them out most willingly—
just what I've been looking for,
the final touch of glory
that our garden needs.

I'm filled up to the brim
with so much giving and receiving
in these few hours,
so much pleasure shared.
The earth, indeed, is full of gifts.

Receiving

Morning scent

Up early
to steal a few moments
in the garden
Pinch back tomato vines
pick up fallen apples
breathe in the beauty
and the cool
before a busy day.

Much later
on the interstate
and far away
a momentary movement
hand to face
brings a scent
that's unmistakable
and I am back again
amid the growing promise
of tomatoes.

Harvest

A great armload of greens
from the garden—
Swiss chard in the pot for dinner
Mint hung up to dry
enough for tea for months to come
Kale and basil chopped for pesto
so tasty and so easy to freeze
A harvest to nourish
body and soul.

Mint

Early spring day
a three year old samples
the garden's delights.

Worms, of course
parsley and celery
survivors of winter,
mint, just coming up.

He pinches at those
little nubs of green
barely poking through the earth
getting just enough
to remind a remembering mouth
of that potent taste.

Loosening

Rain
torrential, unremitting
washed away our porch sale hopes
our efforts all for naught.

The earth that was a fist
so tightly clenched
lies open now and loose.
The weeds I've wrestled with before
bring sweet surprise.
How freely now they yield their hold
responding to the gentlest tug—
from wrestling to partner dance.

Our plans were ruined, but
that richly pliant earth
calls out a song of thanks,
delights my heart.

Sweet potato harvest #1

Mid-October and the sweet potato leaves
have lost their dark green shine
It's time to dig.

I reach through leaves to where the stem
meets earth, push back the soil,
find gold.

Push back some more
and still do not uncover it.
This sweet potato's huge
I dig it out, greater than the size of both my fists
And there's another, and a smaller one
all from one slender cutting with a few new roots
planted in the spring.

And there are more
but I'm filled up
with wonder at the magic of it all
A tiny seed or slip of life
soaks up the elixir
of water, sun and soil
transforms into a richness
more valuable than gold.
The very building blocks of life
are being made
right here before my eyes.

Sweet potato harvest #2

Another year, the weather has turned cold.
The sweet potatoes wait, still in the ground.
I seize an unexpected daylight hour,
take old coat, old gloves, a fork,
a shopping cart of leaves,
go out to dig—
and step into an ancient rite.

It's true I tucked in little slips last spring.
Vines have grown and leaves have multiplied
but who knows what magic
has been working down below?

And so I dig.
Each time I turn the earth
there's treasure to be found.
I straighten to a stunning sunset
spread across the sky
(so easily unnoticed from indoors).

My harvest grows
the colors shift, then fade.
I pile the leaves as cover for the soil,
fill my basket, head for home
as darkness settles.
All is well.

November surprise

Romaine lettuce
in tall stately heads
planted in abundance
at summer's end
with seed gathered last year
and nothing to lose.
Not a surprise this November
but doubly welcome,
still standing fresh and crisp
after the threat of frost.

The surprise
is the peas.
Some of spring's pods
left unpicked
to save for next year's seed,
stood untended,
dried and opened
dropped their treasure,
finally noticed
almost too late.
A hurried scrabble in the earth
to pick them out,
each one a promise
for the year to come.

But some were missed
sprouted and grew
before their time.
Out of season
surely they could never fruit
before the frost.

But purple flowers came
then slivers of tiny pods
that lengthened and started to fill,
gathered in handfuls
this cool November—
a fresh sweet taste to savor,
an unexpected gift
to gladden the heart.

Green and gold

Cook carrots, leeks and greens
bake one big sweet potato
(add a little rice)
feed four.

Breath in the blessing
breathe out thanks
for sun and rain and soil.

Stranger

In the corner of the compost
is a stranger.
Home from far away
I fine the exotic waiting
in my tiny yard.

The compost has never been strange before—
egg shells, vegetable waste
weeds and leaves
the occasional sprouting potato
all familiar as my hand.

Yet this tall foreigner
has boldly taken residence.
Long pointed leaves
dark and shiny
the new ones translucent
almost red—
of royal blood perhaps?
I'm not sure how to behave
in its presence.

I get a pot
prepare it to receive the visitor
and carefully begin to dig.

As I work through layers of waste
I find the seed, key to this mystery.

I am hosting
a mango.

Imagining

Seeing

On my good days
I have an eagle eye for bindweed.
I can spot it
when it's small as a fingernail
new as the day.
I can find the tiniest threads
under a thick clump of yucca or day lily.
Prowling patiently and powerfully through the garden
I see everything.

Other days I get tired
or run out of time.
Then my eye sweeps the plants and the ground
hoping to see less.
Sometimes I catch a glimpse of what might be bindweed
but maybe it's not.
The ones under the yucca and day lily are safe.
I need to be done.

We see what we can afford to see.
The rest we will into invisibility.
Yet I would choose
the eagle eye
patience and power
all the time.

Bees

Of course I know about bees.
They get nectar from flowers
and make honey
and buzz.

This morning
when I came to pull weeds
I found bees
lots of bees
busy in the flowers I had tended all these months—
bees at the trolley tunnel
in the midst of buildings and streets and sidewalks
burying their heads in the flowers
gathering nectar.

It was a miracle—
or maybe not.
Bring earth to what had been bare cement
plant the flowers
tend them
and the bees will come
even here.

Where will they make their honey?
They know better than I.
But now my heart has joined the bees.

The borer

Melons, squashes, pumpkins, cukes—
they just wouldn't grow here.
They sprouted, promising
then withered off
as borers ate the stems.

Forty gardeners tried
and learned the hard way—
no wily strategem was good enough
to beat these bugs.
Yet plots were small and choices big.
We cut our losses,
cultivated other things.

Years passed, one plot devolved to someone new.
She hadn't heard these plants could not be grown—
and baby squash plants sprouted up
naïve, unwarned.

Share the bad news with her
or let nature take its course?
The end would be the same.

And yet, incredibly, they lived,
grew bigger, put out flowers
and then fruit—
a glut of summer squash
bursting with exuberance
completely borer free.

Gardeners' despair
had robbed these insects of
their sustenance
and forced them off the land.
But no one knew.

It took an innocent,
who hadn't heard it was impossible,
to lead the way.

Connection

His farm is in Jamaica
not far outside of Kingston
in the low hills, not the famous higher ones.
Going as often as he can
always on the lookout for cheap flights
he grows so many kinds of fruit that I lose track
—and coffee too.

All this I learn
one morning as I'm heading home
from gardening
basket of produce on my arm.

He'd honked his horn and stopped
leaned over from the driver's seat
said he knew me from my gardening.

He tells his name, and asks me mine
treats me as a peer who knows a common craft.
And so we talk
Omar and Pamela
one farmer to another,
and I walk home
rich in produce on my arm
richer yet in a new friend.

The shovel

I like taking a shovel
on my walk.
It balances lightly in my hand
lending a sense of purpose,
a reminder that
I'm not in this world
just for myself.

Habitat

I thought we were planting
just for beauty--
big bright sunflowers
that call out their glory in August
when others have faded away.

Yet here on a busy street
in a front yard smaller than
a double bed, I find
a goldfinch family has made a home,
a perfect place to tweet
and flit and dine on seeds.

The ones I planted in our common bed
reached for the sun and bloomed
and then grew fat with seeds
Birds came here too, and then,
first day of fall, a squirrel was there
busy with a big seed head
storing up for leaner times.

As one who planted just for beauty
I have learned that sunflowers
have more to give.

Give and take

Give out, take in.

One spring Saturday I gave,
with a work crew at Bartram's Garden
tending their new orchard.
I dug and dug and dug
rooting out the honeysuckle
that was strangling a young tree
whose fruit I may never eat
but which grows our common wealth.

One Sunday, later in the month, I took,
up before dawn to greet the sun
on Easter in the Bartram meadow.
We were enveloped by beauty—
trees, mist, moon, sky—
serenaded by a great bird chorus,
fellow beings who needed no excuse
to celebrate the day,
our job to wonder and be glad.

Give out, take in
like breathing and exhaling
good deep breaths
of clean fresh air.
With only one,
just give or take,
we gasp for life.
We need them both.

Celebrating Easter during a pandemic

The sunrise service that I love,
gathered in a meadow
framed by woods and city skyline,
putting our attention
to the end of night
and the coming of a new day,
was not to be.

Instead, I climbed to our roof—
moon to the west over the great church dome
sunrise to the east, through the skyline—
and settled in to witness
the coming of the light.
And it came.

Back down, my early morning walk
led me round the park
and to the city garden that we share.

Under the peach tree
that I planted years ago
and has yielded so abundantly
I found a tiny seedling poking up—a peach!

As I looked, I kept on finding more—
life in abundance,
unexpected and unearned
ready to grow, to nourish and delight—
an Easter gift to warm the heart.

Fertile ground

In the garden
my mind is fertile.

Ideas that were insubstantial
as dandelion seeds
settle into good earth.

New ways of thinking
push up through the rich soil
poke out into the light.

Conditions in the garden
favor growth.

Pamela Haines, a Philadelphian all her adult life, works in early childhood education and has a passion for the earth and economic integrity. She loves languages, family play, quilting and repair of all kinds, and is closely connected to a community in Northern Uganda.

She has published widely on the skills of peace building and faith and economics. Lead author of *Toward a Right Relationship with Finance: Interest, Debt, Growth and Security,* she has written *Money and Soul* and a new collection of essays entitled *That Clear and Certain Sound.*

<pamelalivinginthisworld.blogspot.com>